United States
Environmental Protection
Agency

January 2013

Rainwater Harvesting

Conservation, Credit, Codes, and Cost
Literature Review and Case Studies

Rainwater Harvesting:

Conservation, Credit, Codes, and Cost

Literature Review and Case Studies

Contact Information

For more information, questions, or comments about this document, contact Chris Solloway at U.S. Environmental Protection Agency, Office of Water, Office of Wetlands, Oceans, and Watersheds, 1200 Pennsylvania Avenue, Mail Code 4503T, Washington, DC 20460, or by email at Solloway.Chris@epamail.epa.gov.

January 2013

EPA-841-R-13-002

Acknowledgements

This document was prepared by the U.S. Environmental Protection Agency (EPA), Office of Water, Office of Wetlands, Oceans, and Watersheds. The EPA Project Manager for this document was Chris Solloway, who provided overall direction and coordination. EPA was supported in the development of this document by The Low Impact Development Center, Inc and Geosyntec Consultants.

TABLE OF CONTENTS

1. INTRODUCTION

Rainwater harvesting has been used throughout history as a water conservation measure, particularly in regions where other water resources are scarce or difficult to access. In recent years, researchers and policy makers have shown renewed interest in water use strategies due to rising water demand, increased interest in conservation (both water and energy), and an increased regulatory emphasis on reducing stormwater runoff volumes and associated pollutant loads. In the last decade, as interest in the practice has grown, numerous state, municipal, and regional agencies have adopted or amended codes and guidelines to encourage responsible and effective rainwater harvesting practices. In addition, researchers from universities and non-government organizations, as well as industry consultants, have published papers and articles addressing a broad range of topics related to the installation, maintenance, costs, and performance of harvest and use systems.

A literature review of existing research and policy documents related to rainwater harvesting has been conducted, with particular focus on characterizing the current state of the practice in the areas of: (1) water conservation, (2) stormwater volume and pollutant load reduction, (3) code and administration considerations and (4) cost factors. The purpose of this report is to summarize the existing knowledge base in these four areas, assess factors affecting economic benefits of rainwater harvesting, and identify topics requiring additional research. This report is not intended to serve as a design document. Readers looking for design guidance should consult a more technically-focused publication, such as the *Texas Manual on Rainwater Harvesting* (TWDB, 2005).

2.   LITERATURE REVIEW SUMMARY

The literature review conducted focused on the impacts of rainwater harvesting in the areas of water conservation, stormwater runoff volume, and pollutant load reduction; code and administration; and cost factors. The review included relevant information for a range of system sizes and complexities from small, passive systems (e.g. rain barrels) to larger systems with fitted pumps, controls, and treatment systems (e.g. active systems or cisterns). For each assessment topic, the primary considerations for literature review were as follows:

Technical – The scientific, engineering, and design elements associated with each topic and how the technical components of a rainwater harvesting system affect performance, compliance, and cost.

- Operation and Maintenance – The practical, day-to-day, and periodic activities and costs associated with effectively operating a rainwater harvesting system.

- Programmatic – The current regulatory environment related to rainwater harvesting, including examples of code modifications, incentive programs, and public outreach.

- Predictability – Reliability of present and future performance of rainwater harvesting systems relative to each assessment topic.

The results of the literature review for each assessment topic are summarized in the following sections.

2.1   Water Conservation

Throughout history, rainwater harvesting has been viewed primarily as a fresh water supply or water conservation practice. In the western United States, conservation continues to serve as a primary driver for rainwater harvesting as the region struggles to meet the water demands of its burgeoning population. This section provides a basic technical description of the two main types of rainwater harvesting systems (passive and active) and outlines the basic maintenance requirements of each. Examples of code requirements and the need for predictability of water demand are also discussed.

2.1.1   Technical

Passive harvesting systems (e.g. rain barrels) are typically small volume (50-100 gallon) systems designed to capture rooftop runoff. Rain barrels are commonly used in residential applications where flow from rain gutter downspouts is easily captured for outdoor uses such as garden and landscape irrigation or car washing. Due to their smaller sizes and ease of siting, passive systems are generally installed at grade, making impact from sunlight on the stored water a consideration. Direct and indirect sunlight will act as a catalyst for algae growth in the cistern, so exposure to sunlight should be limited where possible. Most above-ground cisterns are available in opaque colors or made from opaque materials, and are recommended. Cisterns made of translucent materials such as light colored plastics should be avoided.

Water is extracted from the rain barrels through a spigot typically with no connections to internal or external plumbing. Due to the small volumes and lack of additional treatment, the water collected in rain barrels is not used indoors (even for non-potable uses), and most state and local regulations require clear markings indicating that the water is non-potable. In addition, rain barrels are generally required to be screened to prevent vectors from breeding and secured to avoid creating a drowning hazard. Passive systems are typically designed with an overflow to ground surface or the existing stormwater collection system. The Memorandum of Understanding on permitting requirements for Rainwater Harvesting Systems located within the City and County of San Francisco provides an excellent overview of the design and maintenance requirements for rain barrels and allowable uses for harvested water.

Active harvesting systems (e.g. cisterns) are larger volume (typically 1,000 – 100,000 gallon) systems which capture runoff from roofs or other suitable surfaces (e.g., terraces, walkways, grassed areas and with proper pre-treatment, parking lots), provide water quality treatment, and use pumps or sufficient head[1] to supply water to a distribution system. Cisterns may be made of wood, plastic, metal, or concrete depending on the size and desired location (Hunt and Szpir, 2006). As noted above, cisterns installed at ground surface should be fabricated from opaque materials to limit penetration of light and resulting promotion of algae growth.

Implementation of these systems usually requires significant design effort to: 1) determine optimal cistern sizing based on collection and water demand characteristics, 2) identify suitable cistern locations, 3) engineer piping and related drainage configurations, 4) incorporate water quality treatment, and 5) configure an appropriate distribution system for the harvested water.

Rainwater collected in active systems is typically used for irrigation or for indoor non-potable water replacement (e.g. toilet flushing, clothes washing, evaporative cooling, etc.). The type and complexity of treatment systems depend on the intended use of the harvested water as well as the water quality and permitting requirements in a particular location. Several states – including Georgia, North Carolina, Texas, and Virginia – have produced guidance manuals which provide information about the types of treatment systems and components available for meeting specific water quality objectives. At the municipal level, several major cities – including Los Angeles, San Francisco, Tucson, and Portland – have released guidance and/or policy documents addressing treatment and permitting requirements for rainwater harvesting systems. Treatment devices can range from simple to complex; some examples include first flush diverters, screen filters, ultraviolet light disinfection, ozone treatment, chlorination, and reverse osmosis (TWDB, 2005).

Active rainwater harvesting systems are typically fitted with one or more pumps, electronic water level sensors, system controllers, and water treatment systems and are often supported by municipal or private well water supplies as a back-up water source. These integrated systems are intended to functionally mimic the delivery of domestic water, and are usually connected to back-up supplies through the use of plumbing cross-connections with backflow prevention or air gap based water feeds. The intent of the integrated back-up water supply is to provide uninterrupted water delivery for instances where harvested water is depleted.

This integration prioritizes the use of rainwater before the municipal supply and maximizes its use. When the supply of harvested water runs out, the integrated system automatically switches

---

[1] Large cistern systems located on rooftops or otherwise elevated to provide sufficient driving head to facilitate connections to a distribution system without the need for pumping are also classified as 'Active' systems in this context.

to the municipal supply with little or no disruption in flow. In many areas, state or local regulations restrict the use of cross-connections with mechanical backflow prevention and require that the municipal supply be used to fill small day tanks or to partially refill cisterns directly. In cross-connection configurations, the municipal water feed is directly plumbed to the same water distribution system fed by the harvesting system. It is isolated by automated control valves and passive check valves to prevent the harvested water from flowing into the domestic water supply lines. More positive isolation of these water sources is provided via a backflow prevention device with an internal 'reduced pressure' zone which maintains a lower pressure chamber in the device that obviates flow or suction in the direction opposite normal flow. As such, this device is commonly referred to as a 'reduced pressure zone backflow preventer', an 'RPZ device', or an 'RPZ valve'. Most jurisdictions where RPZ backflow preventers are allowed require the devices be tested periodically. Cross connection regulation is further addressed in this document in the Code and Administration section.

Where cross connection configurations are prohibited, integration of a back-up water supply is provided by partially refilling the cistern or a smaller ancillary day tank, with an air gap at the end of the refill pipe to prevent cross-contamination between the cisterns and the back-up water supply. In such systems, the back-up water supply is triggered (through a level sensor or float-controlled valve) slightly before the cistern or ancillary tank runs out of water, partially refilling the tank to some pre-determined level to ensure supply for applied water demands. Refill designs that provide for refilling of a main cistern versus a day tank will have reduced overall system performance compared to integrated designs with cross-connections because a portion of the storage volume is consumed by municipal water refill, impacting the volume available for harvesting and stormwater control.

The water conservation performance of active systems is significantly better than that of passive systems (e.g. rain barrels) due to two primary factors: storage volumes and delivery systems.

As noted above, passive systems are typically implemented with small volume storage commensurate with catchment areas associated with single roof downspout collection areas. For small systems, the ability to store water between rain events is the most significant factor in a harvesting system's performance. Because of the logistics of collection from distributed roof collection points, small volumes and limited use are almost universally associated with passive systems.

Further limiting the performance of passive systems is the nature of the water delivery system. Since passive systems are by definition not fitted with pumps for pressurizing the water extracted for delivery, their use is usually limited to refilling watering buckets or connection to ground irrigation systems fed over limited distances by gravity. For systems with favorable geometry in terms of elevation and distance to end use locations, these systems can be quite useful. These types of systems are commonly used in the developing world; however, widespread implementation in the United States has been limited.

The demand for potable and non-potable water – and therefore the potential for water conservation – varies significantly with factors such as climate, land use, and development type. Determining appropriate system sizing requires an accurate quantitative analysis of water demand relative to regional precipitation patterns. This is addressed in more detail under the discussion on Predictability.

2.1.2 Operation and Maintenance

In general, passive systems require only minor maintenance at little or no cost to the system owner. The City and County of San Francisco, CA list some basic guidelines for rain barrel maintenance in a 2008 Memorandum of Understanding between the San Francisco Public Utilities Commission, Department of Building Inspection, and Department of Public Health. These guidelines include: keeping rain barrels clear of debris and maintaining all screens and inlet filtration to prevent clogging and vector breeding; annual cleaning of rain barrels with a non-toxic cleaner; clearing debris from the catchment area periodically and using the collected rainwater as soon as possible after each rain event to prevent bacteria growth and provide capacity for capturing the next rain event (City and County of San Francisco, 2008).

Active systems have similar basic maintenance requirements to passive systems, namely debris removal and filter maintenance (City and County of San Francisco, 2008). Because active systems are larger and typically include more components, some additional maintenance may be required depending on the design. For example, most active systems include some type of filtration device or capability upstream of the point of connection of the collection system to the cisterns. Pre-cistern filtration systems, such as filter baskets or vortex filters to capture particulates and gross solids, require periodic maintenance to prevent clogging unless implemented with self-cleaning capability or mechanisms. Cisterns also generally have longer residence times than rain barrels due to their larger storage volumes. As a result, biofilms or aeration devices may be incorporated to prevent algal or bacterial growth (Cabell Brand Center, 2009). Periodic tank inspection is recommended; periodic cleaning and/or disinfection should be performed on an as-needed basis, and should be incorporated into a system maintenance plan in applications where catchment surfaces are exposed to significant debris loading from leaves, trash, pollen, and other elements. Pumps in active systems also require periodic maintenance and replacement. While the exact maintenance requirements depend on the type and configuration of the pump and its usage pattern, general requirements include testing of triggers and float switches and flushing to prevent clogging. The Virginia Rainwater Harvesting Manual provides information on different types of pump configurations and preventive maintenance considerations (Cabell Brand Center, 2009). Finally, fine filtration and water quality adjustment downstream of the pumping system but before distribution piping is common to all but the simplest of outdoor applications, and requires either self-cleaning devices or a periodic maintenance schedule to ensure proper operation of those components.

Inspection and maintenance schedules vary depending on the type of system and the intended use of harvested water. The table below provides guidance on basic maintenance requirements for cistern systems.

Table 1: Suggested Maintenance Procedures for Rainwater Harvesting Systems

Activity	Frequency
Keep gutters and downspouts free of leaves and other debris	O: Twice a year
Inspect and clean pre-screening, inlet filtration devices, and first flush diverters	O: Four times a year
Inspect and clean storage tank lids, paying special attention to vents and screens on inflow and outflow spigots. Check mosquito screens and patch holes or gaps immediately	O: Once a year
Inspect condition of overflow pipes, overflow filter path, and/or secondary runoff reduction practices	O: Once a year
Inspect tank for sediment buildup	I: Every third year
Clear overhanging vegetation and trees over roof surface	I: Every third year
Check integrity of backflow preventer (unless required more frequently by state or local regulations)	I: Every third year
Inspect structural integrity of tank, pump, pipe, and electrical system	I: Every third year
Replace damaged or defective system components	I: Every third year
Key: O = Owner; I = qualified third party Inspector	

Source: Virginia DCR Stormwater Design Specification No. 6 – Rainwater Harvesting

2.1.3 Programmatic

There are currently no federal regulations governing rainwater harvesting for non-potable use, and the policies and regulations enacted at the state and local levels vary widely from one location to another. Regulations are particularly fragmented with regard to water conservation, as the permissible uses for harvested water tend to vary depending on the climate and reliability of the water supply. The level of detail in these regulations also varies from one location to another. In the past, many plumbing codes have not formally defined rainwater harvesting as a practice distinct from water recycling, resulting in more stringent requirements than seemingly necessary. In contrast, cities and counties looking to promote water conservation have begun issuing policies that better define harvested water and its acceptable uses. The City of Portland (Oregon), for example, provides explicit guidance on the accepted uses of harvested water both indoors and outdoors. In January 2010, Los Angeles County issued a policy providing a clear, regulatory definition of "rainfall/non-potable cistern water" and drawing a specific distinction between harvested water and grey or recycled water (County of Los Angeles, 2010). These and other issues are discussed in greater detail in the Code and Administration section.

2.1.4 Predictability

As mentioned previously, the efficacy of a rainwater harvesting system for conserving water depends largely on the ability to balance water demands with the water supply provided by regional precipitation. The ability of a rainwater harvesting system to meet water demands using the supply of available rainwater is typically expressed in terms of Satisfaction (or Utilization) and Reliability (Thomas, 2004; Liaw and Tsai, 2004). Satisfaction refers to the percent of water demands met or projected to be met by the harvesting system over the entire time period analyzed. Reliability refers to the percentage of individual time units (e.g. days) in the time period analyzed that the imposed water demands are entirely met by the system.

Regional climate conditions often play a significant role in determining the reliability of a particular system design. For example, in climates where the majority of rainfall occurs in a single season, systems may be storage-constrained as practical limitations in cistern size prevent storage of sufficient rainfall volume to meet water demand during the dry season. Ideally, on-site use demands would meet or exceed the maximum supply volume over a relatively short duration (TWDB, 2006). In reality, however, matching supply and demand may be quite difficult. The highest performance for a given area will be achieved where water demands imposed on the harvesting system are present contemporaneously with precipitation patterns. Many parts of the eastern U.S., for example, have relatively consistent precipitation patterns across the 12 months of the year. Applying 12-month demands such as toilet water or industrial demands to this rainfall pattern has the potential to realize very strong system performance given proper sizing.

The use of rainwater harvesting systems as a stormwater control measure adds additional complexity as it requires a balance between providing sufficient stored water to meet demands while maintaining adequate cistern capacity to capture anticipated stormwater runoff.

The ability to accurately predict both supply and demand has a significant impact on both the water conservation and stormwater volume reduction performance of harvesting systems. As a result, water usage estimates are often used along with detailed rainfall and climate data to develop a water budget analysis for a particular site. This analysis predicts the water conservation and stormwater runoff reduction performance of a rainwater harvesting system as a function of tank size, and allows for the selection of the optimum cistern size to meet design goals. In comparing discrete rainfall patterns from a particular region with anticipated on-site water demands, water budget analyses also provide a good indication of the efficacy of rainwater harvesting for a particular climate region. Additional information on water budget analysis is provided in the section on Stormwater Runoff Volume and Pollutant Load Reduction.

In developing a water budget analysis, it is necessary to understand the proposed uses for harvested water and the demand rates and patterns associated with those uses. While site-specific data are preferable for system design, a number of studies are available which can provide planning level estimates of water use for different parts of the United States.

The American Water Works Association (AWWA) estimates the average total per capita water use at 172 gallons per capita per day (gpcd), with 101 gpcd coming from outdoor uses, 69.3 gpcd coming from indoor uses and 1.7 gpcd from unknown or unidentified indoor or outdoor use. Residential indoor uses and their respective percentages of total indoor use (69.3 gpcd) are estimated to be: showers (16.8%), clothes washers (21.7%), dishwashers (1.4%), toilets (26.7%), baths (1.7%), leaks (13.7%), faucets (15.7%), and other domestic uses (2.2%) (AWWA, 1999). Of these, toilets and clothes washers have been suggested as ideal potable demand replacements using either reclaimed greywater or harvested rainwater, which could supply up to a total of approximately 48.3% of the total typical demand (Hunt and Szpir, 2006; Gold et al, 2010).

The Pacific Institute has published similar data based on a study of water use in California; in addition to residential use, this study also considers water use at commercial, industrial, and institutional facilities (Pacific Institute, 2003). Section 4 of the Pacific Institute Report provides a detailed discussion of end uses of water in the commercial, industrial, and institutional (CII) sector. The study considers a broad range of development types, including hospitals, hotels, office buildings, and manufacturing facilities. For the CII sector as a whole, end uses and their respective percentages of total use are provided as follows: landscaping (35%), kitchen (6%), cooling (15%), restroom (16%), process (17%), laundry (2%), and other (9%). Toilet flushing is estimated to account for 72% of restroom water use in the CII sector (Pacific Institute, 2003). It should be noted that these values represent averages over a variety of development types. The figure below summarizes the proportion of total water use attributed to different end uses as a function of development type.

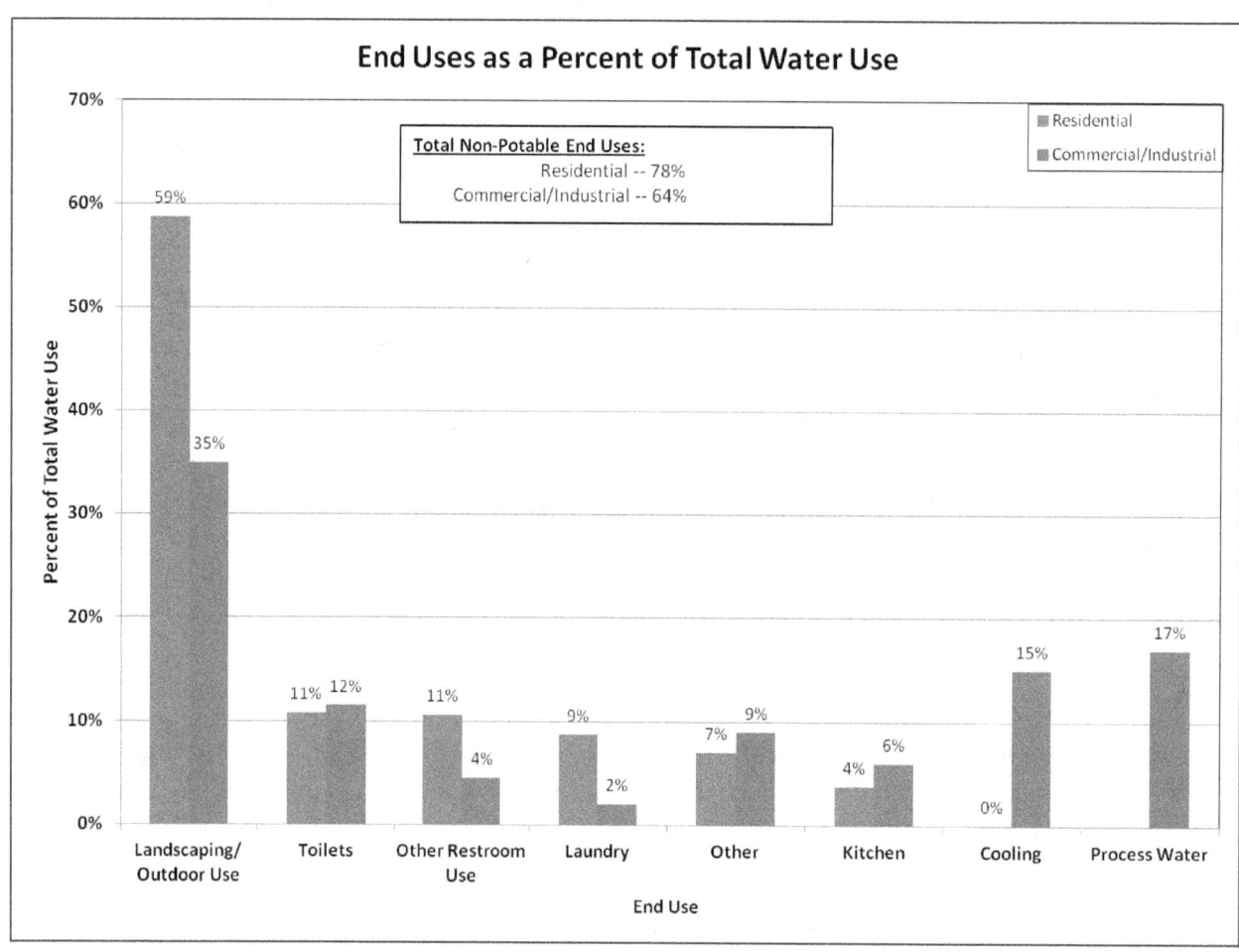

1 – Residential end uses based on AWWA (1999).

2 -- Commercial/Industrial end uses based on Pacific Institute (2003).

The AWWA has also published water usage estimates for a variety of commercial and industrial development types (AWWA, 2000). These data show separate estimates for different end use types based on studies conducted in several cities across the U.S. The differences in these estimates may be significant based on climate and other regional factors. Schools in Phoenix, for example, spend a significantly higher proportion of total water use on landscape irrigation (54%) as compared to Denver (29%). Morales et al. present an alternative method for estimating water use at commercial, industrial, and institutional facilities based on heated building area and other parcel-level attributes (Morales, 2009). Additional resources for water usage estimates are provided in the Recommended Resources at the end of this section.

The significant proportion of water use attributed to non-potable uses demonstrate the potential for water conservation benefits through rainwater harvesting. It should be noted, however, that the data presented here are average values, which may be subject to significant variability, and should not be used in lieu of site-specific data for individual harvesting system designs.

Water Conservation -- Links to Recommended Resources

Codes and Policy Documents:
    City and County of San Francisco:
        Rainwater Harvesting in San Francisco

Guidance Documents:
    Texas Water Development Board:
        The Texas Manual on Rainwater Harvesting, 3rd Edition

    Georgia Department of Community Affairs:
        Georgia Rainwater Harvesting Guidelines

Research Documents:
    Water Use Statistics:
        American Water Works Association (AWWA):
        Commercial and Institutional End Uses of Water
        Residential End Uses of Water

    Pacific Institute:
        Waste Not, Want Not: The Potential for Urban Water Conservation in California

---

2.2   Stormwater Runoff Volume and Pollutant Load Reduction

In addition to providing a water conservation benefit, rainwater harvesting systems are also recognized as a Low Impact Development (LID) technique for stormwater management. By retaining stormwater runoff for on-site use, harvesting systems reduce the runoff volumes and pollutant loads entering the stormwater collection system, helping to restore pre-development hydrology and mitigate downstream water quality impacts. As a result, many state and local governments have begun to encourage the use of rainwater harvesting as a stormwater Best Management Practice (BMP). This section discusses the technical design and operational considerations associated with the use of rainwater harvesting for stormwater management, provides an overview of some regulatory and incentive programs for stormwater runoff reduction, and outlines methods for maintaining available storage volume to ensure reliable performance.

2.2.1 Technical

While passive rainwater harvesting systems can be fairly easy to implement (as discussed previously), they present limited opportunity for significant reduction in stormwater runoff due to their relatively small volume, and an inability to ensure that stormwater retention volume is available at the onset of precipitation events. These limitations lead to the need for strong outreach campaigns and dissemination of operational guidance with deployment of these systems, as well as widespread implementation in order to achieve the significant stormwater flow reduction benefits. City-wide green initiatives, such as those undertaken in New York and Los Angeles, have attempted to address the need for widespread implementation by sponsoring rain barrel giveaways and engaging the public using new and social media. Public education about the stormwater benefits of rainwater harvesting and the importance of managing storage volume through responsible and reliable water demand is a significant step toward improving the stormwater performance of passive systems.

Unlike rain barrels, well-designed active harvesting systems can provide greater flexibility for managing stormwater runoff because they are sized based on an analysis of local precipitation and site-specific demand. Tank sizing for stormwater performance requires a detailed water budget analysis which considers the size of the catchment area, local precipitation patterns and anticipated indoor and outdoor water use. While some guidance manuals recommend use of monthly average precipitation data in cistern sizing, these data fail to capture the discrete size and distributional characteristics of shorter daily or intra-daily rainfall events which have significant implications for stormwater performance.

A better approach is to use a long-term, continuous record of hourly or daily precipitation data (available from the National Climatic Data Center) for a given location (Cabell Brand Center, 2009). The continuous record of precipitation can be analyzed in a spreadsheet model along with anticipated demands to provide more precise estimates of water conservation and stormwater performance as a function of cistern volume for a given catchment area and demand scenario. The designer can use the results to identify the most cost effective sizing option that meets the design goals.

The effectiveness of a rainwater harvesting system for managing stormwater runoff depends on the presence of a consistent and reliable demand that can be used to drawdown the cisterns and to ensure adequate volume for stormwater retention. The state of Virginia's 2011 design specification for rainwater harvesting provides specific guidelines for ensuring reliable demand and offers a robust methodology for cistern sizing based on analysis of the 30-year continuous rainfall record and anticipated demand scenarios (VA DCR, 2011). The analysis outlined in the Virginia DCR specification focuses on establishing a runoff reduction credit based on the percent of runoff volume from storms less than or equal to a target storm of 1" that is retained on site through the use of rainwater harvesting. VA DCR has developed a Cistern Design Spreadsheet as a companion to the specification that can be used to estimate the anticipated performance of the system. The figure below is an example output from the spreadsheet showing the runoff reduction credit and overflow frequency as a function of cistern size. An optimal cistern size may be determined based on the location of the "knee" of the curve, commonly perceived as a point of diminishing return, beyond which incremental additional storage volume has a smaller incremental effect on stormwater runoff reduction (Forasté and Hirschman, 2010).

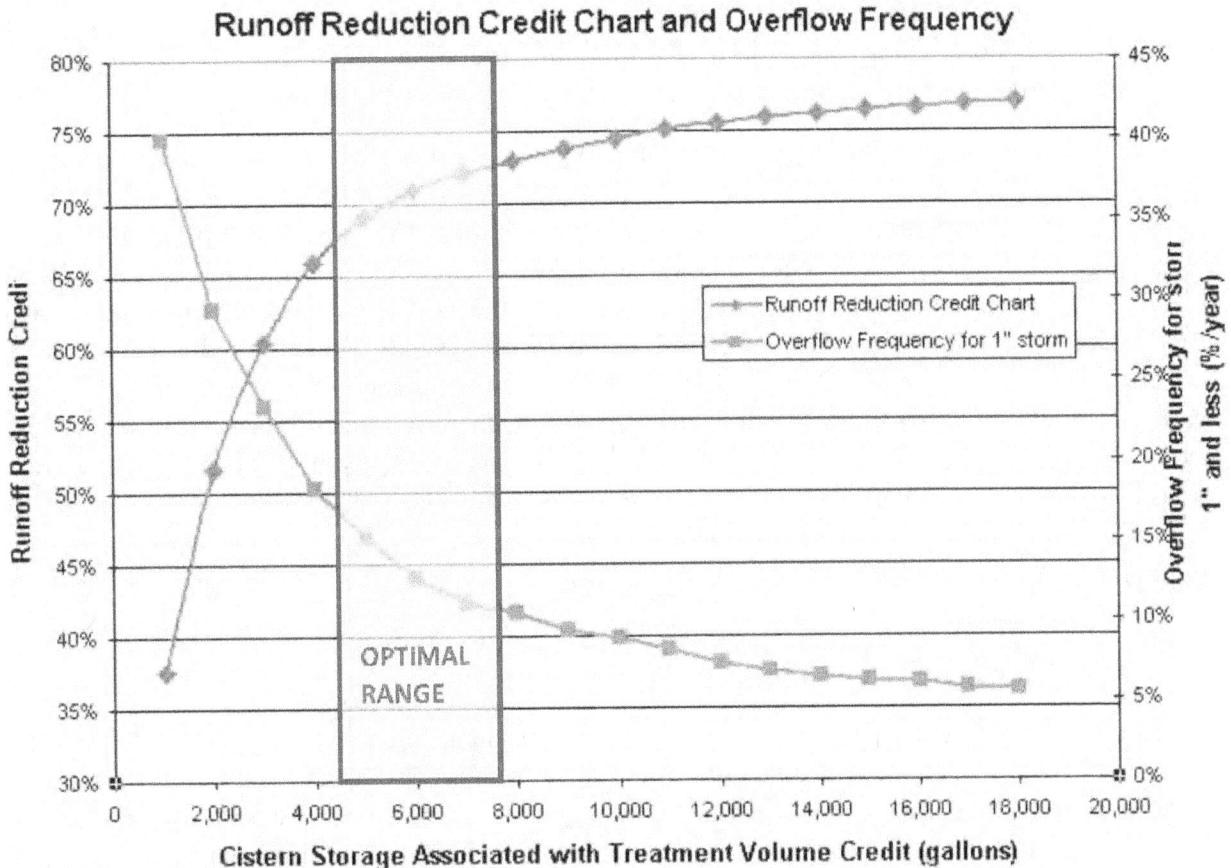

Source: Forasté and Hirschman (2010). A Methodology for Using Rainwater Harvesting as a Stormwater Management BMP. Conference Proceedings, 2010 Low Impact Development Conference.

In addition to regional precipitation patterns, stormwater performance of rainwater harvesting systems is also heavily dependent on the presence of consistent, year-round demands to drawdown the cisterns. Both the Virginia and North Carolina rainwater harvesting guidelines require systems to have a dedicated, year-round use (VA DCR 2011; NC DWQ, 2008). Where anticipated cistern demand includes seasonal demand, such as irrigation, infiltration or other on-site practices must be used during non-irrigation months to ensure adequate drawdown rates. In Virginia, for example, harvesting systems may be combined with other runoff reduction practices, such as rain gardens, filter strips, or underground infiltration basins, installed downstream of the cisterns. During periods of low demand, a low level orifice may be used to "gradually drawdown [tanks] at a specified design rate between storm events" to ensure that the tanks have adequate volume for upcoming storm events. However, the intent is not for the system to operate as a detention facility and the typical flows associated with drawdown are far smaller than those associated with detention facilities (VA DCR, 2011). The water is discharged to the downstream controls which are engineered to infiltrate the design flow rate. This approach is particularly useful in areas where irrigation occurs during only part of the year. In these areas, infiltration practices provide a means of restoring available tank volume during non-irrigation months in the absence of other water demands (VA DCR, 2011; Forasté and Hirschman, 2010).

Real-time controls are an emerging technology in the field of rainwater harvesting and stormwater management. These systems utilize recently developed hardware and software solutions to allow for dynamic control of harvesting systems to achieve optimized stormwater control benefits. Real-time rainwater harvesting control systems are equipped with internet-connected logic controllers which are used to monitor the volume of water in the cisterns and data from weather forecasts in real time to affect the release timing of stored water.

The controller compares the available volume in the cistern to the volume anticipated to be captured from the forecasted rain event. By releasing water prior to rain events, the system maximizes runoff capture, thereby reducing discharge volumes, attenuating peak flows, and enhancing water quality treatment. This is particularly beneficial in combined sewer system (CSS) watersheds. By releasing stored water prior to the rain event and maximizing storage volume for an imminent rainfall event, these advanced systems can be used to reduce and prevent combined sewer overflows (CSOs) from occurring. In non-CSS areas, the release of water during dry weather helps to attenuate peak flows, thereby reducing erosion potential and geomorphic impacts on receiving streams. These stormwater benefits are realized with minimal impact on the supply of harvested water. Through the use of real-time controls, a smaller cistern volume can be used to realize the same stormwater benefits as a much larger system. Pilot scale research on real-time control technologies is ongoing and the exact benefits at the site scale have yet to be quantified.

2.2.2 Operation and Maintenance

As mentioned previously, passive systems rely on consistent, manual water use to deplete the rain barrel and make volume available for capturing the next rain event. San Francisco encourages rain barrel owners to use collected rainwater as soon as possible after each rain event for optimal performance (City and County of San Francisco, 2008). If stormwater management is of primary concern, it may be beneficial to create additional demands for harvested water outside of conventional uses such as car washing or lawn irrigation. As part of its rain barrel program, the City of Los Angeles promotes the creation of rain gardens which can be used to infiltrate rainwater on residential properties. As part of regular maintenance, owners anticipating imminent rainfall can empty rain barrels into these areas in the absence of other water demands.

Unlike rain barrels, active harvesting systems are typically sized with some consideration for stormwater performance during the design phase, eliminating the need for tank emptying as part of maintenance activities. The primary maintenance considerations for cisterns involve cleaning of filters and tanks and inspection of equipment, as previously discussed (see the Operation and Maintenance portion of the Water Conservation section).

2.2.3 Programmatic

State and local codes and regulations typically do not address the use of rain barrels for stormwater management. However, a number of major cities throughout the country, including New York, Los Angeles, Portland (Oregon), Philadelphia, and Chicago have implemented programs to encourage the use of rain barrels and to educate the public on the stormwater benefits of rainwater harvesting. In some cases, municipalities have invested in the purchase of rain barrels for distribution to individual homeowners, while others offer rebates for rain barrel purchases. These programs are generally included in larger green initiatives which are well-publicized by the sponsoring entity or entities. Such programs help to build understanding and encourage widespread use of passive harvesting systems.

In the past, many program managers did not know how to account for the water quantity and quality benefits of rainwater harvesting. Because credit was not granted, use of the practice as a stormwater management BMP was very limited in many localities. To address this, a number of states and municipalities have adopted policies and tools to grant the practice credit in order to put it on a level playing field with other BMPs (Forasté and Hirschman, 2010).

As mentioned previously, the state of Virginia's updated rainwater harvesting design specification, adopted in March 2011, provides a good example of a method for quantifying the stormwater runoff volume and pollutant load reduction benefits of harvesting systems (VA DCR, 2011). Historically, many regulations have focused on percent removal as the primary metric for assigning water quality treatment credit to BMPs. The Virginia specification, however, is representative of an increasing trend toward the development of stormwater regulations that recognize the water quality benefits associated with volume reduction. Other states, including North Carolina, have adopted similar policies, and the Energy Independence and Security Act of 2007 (EISA) – regulating stormwater management at federal facilities – also emphasizes volume reduction as an effective stormwater management strategy. Other stormwater regulations, including Total Maximum Daily Load (TMDL) requirements for receiving water bodies, place additional emphasis on the need for volume reduction.

Rather than focusing solely on percent removal as a metric for assigning water quality treatment credit for BMPs, these regulations recognize that for a given concentration, the mass of a pollutant that is discharged to receiving waters is directly related to the amount of volume discharged. Therefore, a reduction in stormwater volume discharge also corresponds to a reduction in pollutant loading. As regulators place increasing emphasis on volume reduction, rainwater harvesting is likely to gain more widespread acceptance as an effective stormwater management BMP.

It should be noted that while a number of regulators have recognized the importance of volume reduction in stormwater performance of BMPs, the metrics that have been proposed for quantifying volume reduction vary. EISA, for example, requires BMPs to be sized for full on-site retention of runoff generated from the 95th percentile storm event, and many state and MS4 regulations have similar event-based requirements. In some cases, the metric of interest is based on long-term volume reductions determined from continuous simulation modeling or on a comparison to pre-development hydrology. Whether specified in terms of event-based or long-term requirements, procedures for designing a rainwater harvesting system to comply with these standards are similar and involve the use of a water budget analysis as described in Section 2.2.1.

In response to the increased emphasis on volume reduction in stormwater regulations at the federal and state levels, many municipalities have recognized the need for dedicated resources to address stormwater quantity and quality. A number of cities have created stormwater utilities and changed fee structures to explicitly identify a stormwater fee separate from traditional water supply and sewer charges. To incentivize on-site stormwater management, several cities— including Louisville and Philadelphia – offer stormwater credits or fee reductions to property owners who utilize BMPs to reduce runoff volumes. Some municipalities, including New York City, have also sponsored grant programs to fund pilot projects that demonstrate the efficacy of using rainwater harvesting to achieve broader goals for CSO reduction and water quality improvement.

2.2.4 Predictability

As discussed above, passive systems have little predictability for stormwater control due to their limited storage volumes and the inability to project when or to what extent storage is available to accept additional runoff. For active systems, providing consistent demand to ensure regular use of the stored volume is essential to maximizing the effectiveness of rainwater harvesting as a stormwater control. Well-designed cistern systems use water budget analyses (as described in Section 2.2.1) to inform the selection of a tank volume that will optimize stormwater performance. These analyses consider both precipitation and demand patterns in selecting an appropriate cistern volume. By enforcing requirements for year-round demand and establishing well-defined criteria for achieving stormwater credit, state regulations, such as those in Virginia and North Carolina, can help to make stormwater performance of rainwater harvesting systems more predictable.

Stormwater Runoff Volume and Pollutant Load Reduction -- Links to Recommended Resources

Codes and Policy Documents:

Rainwater Harvesting and Stormwater Management Regulations

Virginia Department of Conservation and Recreation:

> *Design Specification No. 6: Rainwater Harvesting*

North Carolina Department of Water Quality:

> *Technical Guidance: Stormwater Treatment Credit for Rainwater Harvesting*

Guidance Documents

US EPA:

> *Technical Guidance on Implementing the Stormwater Runoff Requirements for Federal Projects under Section 438 of the Energy Independence and Security Act*

Cabell Brand Center:

> *Virginia Rainwater Harvesting Manual, 2nd Edition*

Research Documents:

ASCE Low Impact Development Conference (Forasté and Hirschman):
> *A Methodology for Using Rainwater Harvesting as a Stormwater Management BMP*

2.3 Code and Administration

Although rainwater harvesting has been widely promoted for its water conservation and stormwater benefits, there has been little consensus among regulators regarding plumbing and maintenance requirements or the permissible uses of harvested water. As a result, few codes have been developed to address these issues. The majority of regulations that do exist have been enacted at the state and local level; the system requirements and level of detail provided in these codes and ordinances varies from one location to another. This section provides an overview of the regulatory environment at the federal, state, and local levels with regard to the technical and operational aspects of rainwater harvesting systems.

2.3.1 Technical

National and International Codes: Until the fall of 2010, neither the national Uniform Plumbing Code (UPC) nor International Plumbing Code (IPC) directly addressed rainwater harvesting in their potable or stormwater sections (Kloss, 2008; Traugott, 2007; Ecker, 2007). In some cases, harvested rainwater was regulated as reclaimed water, which can lead to confusion, over-burdensome requirements, and discourage or prohibit the use of rainwater harvesting.

In 2010, the International Association of Plumbing and Mechanical Officials (IAPMO) published the first of its kind *Green Plumbing and Mechanical Code Supplement (GPMCS)*. The supplement is a separate document from the Uniform Plumbing and Mechanical Codes and establishes requirements for green building and water efficiency applicable to plumbing and mechanical systems.

Green Plumbing and Mechanical Code Support

In 2010, the International Association of Plumbing and Mechanical Officials (IAPMO) published the first of its kind *Green Plumbing and Mechanical Code Supplement (GPMCS)*. The supplement is a separate document from the Uniform Plumbing and Mechanical Codes and establishes requirements for green building and water efficiency applicable to plumbing and mechanical systems.

The document was created "to bridge the gap between existing plumbing and mechanical codes and green building programs" and includes sections on:

- Water Efficiency and Conservation
- Alternate Water Source Usage
- Water Heating Systems
- Energy Efficiency for HVAC Systems
- Enhanced Environmental Quality for Buildings

The GPMCS also "serves as a repository for provisions that ultimately will be integrated into the Uniform Codes" (IAPMO, 2010).

According to IAPMO, the entire section of the GPMCS on Alternate Water Source Usage will be included in the 2012 edition of the Uniform Plumbing Code (IAPMO, 2011).

Additional information on the GPMCS can be found at: http://www.iapmo.org/pages/iapmo_green.aspx

---

The purpose of the GPMCS is to "provide a set of technically sound provisions that encourage sustainable practices and works towards enhancing the design and construction of plumbing and mechanical systems that result in a positive long-term environmental impact" (IAPMO, 2010).

While making recommendations on a wide range of water efficiency design methods and tactics, the document does not seek jurisdiction of items addressed in the Supplement: rather, it refers throughout to the "Authority Having Jurisdiction" and existing codes for matters related to permitting and approvals.

In addressing "Non-potable Rainwater Catchment Systems", the GPMCS specifically identifies provisions for collection surfaces, storage structures, drainage, pipe labeling, use of potable water as a back-up supply (provided by air-gap only), and a wide array of other design and construction criteria. It also refers to and incorporates information from the *ARCSA/ASPE Rainwater Catchment Design and Installation Standard*, a document published in 2008 under a joint effort by the American Rainwater Catchment Systems Association (ARCSA) and the American Association of Plumbing Engineers (ASPE).

Also, NSF International has a Task Group on Onsite Residential and Commercial Greywater Treatment Systems focused on adopting guidelines and standards for the evaluation of on-site use and reuse systems for greywater, blackwater, rainwater, and stormwater. An initial product of this work is the NSF/ANSI 350: Onsite Residential and Commercial Reuse Treatment Systems American national standard. While much of the subject matter is beyond the scope of this document, it is important to note that certifying an on-site use system for NSF/ANSI 350 also satisfies requirements for leading green building programs such as LEED Building Design & Construction 2012 Draft Standard and the National Association of Home Builders National Green Building certification program. Further, examples of fully integrated harvesting and wastewater treatment system are being built to explore the benefits of combining natural systems for runoff reduction and onsite treatment. One such example is a system at The Rodale Institute's Water Purification Eco-Center or WPEC, where a visitor's center incorporates restrooms that use rainwater for sewage conveyance and constructed wetlands as a safe and eco-friendly alternative to traditional septic systems (www.rodaleinstitute.org/wpec/home).

Professional Standards: The purpose of the *ARCSA/ASPE Rainwater Catchment Design and Installation Standard* is to "assist engineers, designers, plumbers, builders, developers, local government, and users in safely implementing a rainwater catchment system. It applies to new rainwater catchment installations, alterations, additions, maintenance, and repairs to existing installations" (ARCSA/ASPE, 2008). This document discusses the general components of rainwater harvesting systems and provides guidance on a range of applications, including non-potable, potable, and fire protection.

Other professional organizations in the construction industry have also started to address rainwater harvesting as it relates to green building design. For example, the American Society of Heating, Refrigerating, and Air-Conditioning Engineers (ASHRAE) has added a section on water efficiency to the latest edition of its *ASHRAE GreenGuide*, which is intended as an "easy-to-use reference" for green building design. The introduction of the GPMCS and NSF/ANSI 350, along with these professional standards, holds promise of significant impact on the design and construction industries associated with the implementation of harvesting systems, although their penetration to date in these fields is tough to ascertain. Once adopted by local permitting authorities on a widespread basis, they should allow for a more uniform and robust design and installation industry to emerge.

State Guidance and Regulations: At the state level, the amount of regulation for rainwater harvesting varies widely from state to state. A number of states, including Texas, Georgia, and Virginia have developed guidance manuals, with several more under development, for rainwater harvesting and are generally supportive of the practice. In general, state code provisions allow for more stringent policies than those provided on the federal level, but not less. With the publication of the GPMCS, states will now have a new benchmark from which to establish their policies.

In 2006, prior to the publication of the GPMCS, the Texas Water Development Board, along with other state agencies, created the Texas Rainwater Harvesting Committee to "establish recommended standards for the domestic use of harvested rainwater, including health and safety standards [and] to develop standards for collection methods" (TWDB, 2006). This committee submitted a set of recommendations to the Texas State Legislature which would help to shape future legislation and create a more formal policy for the collection and use of harvested rainwater. Other states have followed Texas's lead in addressing the need for rainwater harvesting legislation. However, progress has been slow; as of 2010, only ten states had policies or laws specifically addressing rainwater harvesting, and the laws that have been passed often fail to address key issues such as plumbing requirements and permissible uses of harvested water (Gold et al, 2010).

With increasing emphasis on green building practices and the call for water and energy efficiency among those in the construction community, more states are beginning to address the need for rainwater harvesting legislation. The Illinois State Senate, for example, introduced a bill in February 2011 that would define "rainwater harvesting distribution system" and "rainwater harvesting collection system" in the Illinois Plumbing Code and require the Illinois Department of Health to establish minimum standards for rainwater harvestings systems by 2012 (Illinois State Senate, 2011). This example is indicative of a growing trend at the state level encouraging the use and proper regulation of rainwater harvesting systems.

Existing regulations tend to vary widely in scope and focus. Some states, such as Texas, have focused on rainwater harvesting as a water conservation practice; others, such as North Carolina, have more structured regulations for rainwater harvesting as a stormwater control measure. More coordination between state Department of Health agencies, building commissioners and code organizations, and regional stormwater managers is necessary to aid in the development of more comprehensive regulations to address all aspects of rainwater harvesting.

Municipal and Local Policies: Municipal and local regulations are more difficult to track, but a number of examples of rainwater harvesting ordinances or code changes at the municipal level were discovered in the course of this study. Tucson, Arizona, for example, has passed a law requiring 50% of a commercial property's irrigation water to be supplied from rainwater beginning in June 2010. In 2008, Albuquerque-Bernalillo County in New Mexico began requiring rainwater harvesting to capture at least 85% of rooftop runoff for all new homes (Kloss, 2008).

A Broader Look: International Examples of Rainwater Harvesting Regulations

The issue of developing effective rainwater harvesting legislation is not limited to the continental United States. There are many countries and territories, including the US Virgin Islands, Australia, and Singapore, that have embraced the practice to encourage conservation, satisfy water demands, or treat stormwater runoff. Below are examples of the type of progressive legislation enacted in these areas to promote the use of rainwater harvesting.

St. Thomas, US Virgin Islands: In St. Thomas, developers are required to incorporate rainwater harvesting systems into all residential site plans in order to obtain a residential building permit. This approach differs from most U.S. regulations, which are structured to incentivize rainwater harvesting but do not require it. Harvested water is used mainly for non-potable applications.

City of Salisbury, Australia: The city of Salisbury has implemented a centralized, city-wide harvesting system linked to the city's existing storm sewer. Runoff is collected and stored centrally, treated, and then used for groundwater recharge, enabling the city to limit discharges to marine resources while replenishing the water supply. This approach is somewhat similar to the "storm tunnels" used for temporary detention in many combined sewer areas in the U.S., but the concept of retaining the stored water for recharge purposes rather than simple detention is innovative.

Singapore: In Singapore, rooftop runoff is collected from almost all buildings and re-used for non-potable purposes. Road runoff is also collected into reservoirs and filtered prior to re-use in non-potable applications. This approach differs from that used in many U.S. communities where runoff from non-roof surfaces is often restricted due to water quality concerns. These concerns are justified, and the advisability of non-roof collection depends on the level of treatment and the desired end use.

Additional information on these and other examples of rainwater harvesting practices in international communities can be found in *Stormwater Non-Potable Beneficial Uses and Effects on Urban Infrastructure* (Pitt, et al 2011). Available at:

http://www.iwapublishing.com/template.cfm?name=isbn9781780400365

In addition to encouraging (or even requiring) rainwater harvesting, several local authorities have also implemented policies outlining requirements for the design, inspection, and approved uses of harvesting systems. The previously mentioned Memorandum of Understanding passed by the City and County of San Francisco defines specific roles for the Public Utilities Commission, Department of Building and Inspection and Department of Public Health with regard to regulation of rainwater harvesting systems. The document was issued after the City amended its plumbing code to allow for rainwater harvesting and provides a thorough description of the technical and permitting requirements for rainwater harvesting in San Francisco (City and County of San Francisco, 2008). Los Angeles County issued a similar policy in January 2010 "to establish standardized procedures for the review and approval of plans and specifications" for rainwater harvesting systems and "to provide guidelines for the approved use and operational practices for any proposed system prior to implementation" (County of Los Angeles, 2010). Policies such as these are good examples of a proactive approach to stormwater use regulation. In the absence of policy, there is often confusion and a tendency to err on the side of unnecessarily restricting use, rather than encouraging it. Establishing guidelines for the installation, permitting, and operation of harvesting systems alleviates confusion and can lead to wider use of the practice, which may be particularly beneficial in arid areas of the western and southwestern United States.

2.3.2 Operation and Maintenance

While several states' guidance manuals contain sections describing recommended maintenance practices, few states or municipalities have enacted laws or codes governing the maintenance of harvesting systems. The primary reason for this lack of regulation is the lack of available resources to enforce such regulations.

Many rainwater harvesting policies also fail to provide detailed information on the operation of rainwater harvesting systems and accepted uses of harvested water. "Harvested stormwater has most often been used for irrigation purposes, but policies are changing to allow rainwater to be used for indoor water use where it can meet a significant portion of non-potable water demands" (Gold et al, 2010). As discussed previously, the AWWA estimated that over 78% of domestic water use goes to non-potable uses (AWWA, 1999). The Pacific Institute provided a similar estimate (76%) for office buildings, and data for the CII sector indicate an average of 64% of water may be attributed to non-potable uses (Pacific Institute, 2003). Water from a municipal supply or drinking water well is typically treated to drinking water standards, even when it is used to satisfy non-potable demands.

Development of regulations that match the required level of treatment to the intended use would allow for the use of harvested rainwater (with minimal on-site treatment) as a viable, low-cost alternative to the drinking water supply for non-potable uses. In countries such as India, Germany, and Australia, where rainwater harvesting has gained wide acceptance, additional efforts have been made to address the need to identify the specific end uses for which use of harvested water is appropriate. The table below provides an example of a framework used in Australia to identify the residential and commercial non-potable uses for which harvested water may be substituted for municipal water. This framework acknowledges differences in required water quality and treatment depending on development type, end use, and collection surface.

Key: ○ Acceptable   ● Possible   ○ Not recommended   ▨ Not applicable

	Domestic (rainwater)	Commercial	
		Rainwater (from roof only)	Stormwater (roof and ground)
Amenities/ Bathroom	●	○	○
Kitchen/ Food Prep.	●	●	○
Hot Water System	○	○	○
Toilet flushing	○	○	●
Laundry	○	○	●
Irrigation/Garden	○	○	○
Vehicle/Gear Washing	○	○	○
Cooling Tower	▨	○	○
Pool Top Up Water	○	○	○
Other Process Water	▨	○	●

Source: Hauber-Davidson, G. Supplementing Urban Water Supplies Through Industrial and Commercial Rainwater Harvesting Schemes. Water Conservation Group, Pymble/Sydney NSW, Australia. <www.watergroup.com.au/download/P_RWH-integrUrbWatSuplyGHDv1a070308.pdf>. (Accessed June 2012).

A similar level of detail is needed in U.S. regulations to remove ambiguity, address barriers to implementation, and increase the potential benefits of rainwater harvesting as a water conservation practice.

The City of Portland (Oregon) One and Two Family Dwelling Specialty Code for rainwater harvesting serves is one example of a code at the local level that addresses this need by specifying the acceptable uses of harvested rainwater both indoors and outdoors and prescribing methods for building an approved system that ensures that harvested rainwater stays separate from potable water (City of Portland, 2001). Similar regulations enacted at the local, state, and federal levels would promote the use of rainwater harvesting by giving property owners confidence that their efforts to conserve water resources are both approved and safe.

Stormwater Pollution and Rainwater Harvesting

In recent years, the potential for contamination of stormwater runoff with pollutants originating from point and non-point sources has been a topic of increasing interest for stormwater engineers and water resource managers and has played a prominent role in the development of stormwater regulations designed to protect public health and receiving water quality. This increased focus on water quality improvement has also prompted researchers to seek to better understand the sources of pollution which may be found on roofs and other surfaces.

Understanding the sources of stormwater pollution is particularly important to the practice of rainwater harvesting to prevent health risks or unnecessary distribution of pollutants. The body of existing research contains a number of studies related to the potential for contamination of runoff from commonly used roofing materials. The table below provides several examples of materials that have the potential to contribute pollutants to rainwater and recommended, safe end uses for water harvested from these surfaces.

Roofing Material	Pollutants of Concern	Suitable end uses
Asphalt shingles	Lead, Mercury	Contaminants vary by product. Sample water quality prior to use.
Galvanized metal	Cadmium, Nickel, Zinc, Phosphorus	Contaminants vary by product. Sample water quality prior to use.
Green roof	Nutrients, COD	Suitable for irrigation and other non-potable end uses.
Copper flashing, downspouts	Copper	Not suitable for human consumption, including drinking water, vegetable gardening, or swimming pools.
Lead flashing, solder	Lead	Not suitable for human consumption, including drinking water, vegetable gardening, or swimming pools.
Wood shingle	Copper, Arsenic, Nutrients	Not recommended for rainwater harvesting.
Cement and terra cotta tiles	Lead, Copper, Cadmium, Bacteria, Asbestos	Not recommended for rainwater harvesting.
Aluminum roofing	none	All uses
Rubber membrane	none	All uses

In areas where rainwater collection from non-roof surfaces is permitted, runoff should be monitored for contaminants of concern, such as metals, oil, and grease and any site-specific parameters before harvesting is implemented.

Additional information on stormwater pollution and rainwater harvesting can be found in the Recommended Resources listed at the end of this section.

Codes and Administration -- Links to Recommended Resources

Codes and Policy Documents:

Plumbing and Mechanical Codes

International Association of Plumbing and Mechanical Officials (IAPMO):
   Green Plumbing and Mechanical Code Supplement

International Code Council:
   2012 International Plumbing Code

Research Documents:

ASCE Low Impact Development Conference (Gold et al, 2010):
   Rainwater Harvesting: Policies, Programs, and Practices for Water Sustainability

US EPA (Kloss, 2007):
   Managing Wet Weather with Green Infrastructure: Municipal Handbook on Rainwater Harvesting

Water Environment Research Foundation (WERF) (Pitt et al. 2011):
   Stormwater Non-Potable Beneficial Uses and Effects on Urban Infrastructure

Journal of Irrigation and Drainage Engineering (Clark, et al. 2008):
   Roofing Materials' Contributions to Stormwater Runoff Pollution

United States Geological Survey (Van Metre and Mahler, 2003):
   The Contribution of Particles From Rooftops to Contaminant Loading to Urban Streams

2.4   Cost Factors

A perceived lack of economic benefit is often cited as a barrier to more widespread implementation of rainwater harvesting systems. High upfront costs and easy access to low-cost municipal or private water sources in much of the United States has led some to discount the water conservation benefits of stormwater capture and on-site use. However, recent trends in water demand and water prices, coupled with the growing number of regulatory and economic incentives for stormwater management, indicate a need for a more detailed cost-benefit analysis of harvesting systems. This section provides a discussion of the factors affecting capital and maintenance costs of rainwater harvesting systems along with an overview of water rate structures and the argument for "full cost" pricing of water. The required elements of a detailed cost-benefit analysis are outlined, including factors affecting the monetary value of each cost or benefit.

2.4.1 Technical

Passive systems typically represent a "low-tech" and low cost option for rainwater harvesting and on-site use. As mentioned previously, a number of cities have distributed rain barrels to homeowners as part of green initiatives to promote rainwater harvesting while others offer rebates or coupons for rain barrel purchases. Rain barrels range in price depending on the size and material; a typical 50-gallon, plastic rain barrel with a spigot and overflow can be purchased from a hardware store or online retailer for around $70.

Costs for active rainwater harvesting systems vary widely depending on the size and complexity of the system. For simple systems, which collect water from roof areas and do not require large media or vortex filters, the storage volume is the primary driver of system cost. Cisterns range in price depending on the material, size, and shape but costs are typically between $1.50 and $3.00 per gallon of storage, with per gallon costs generally decreasing with increasing tank size. Additional costs are incurred for filtration, pumps, distribution systems, excavation (if cisterns are placed underground), distribution plumbing and drainage connections, installation, and other components. These costs may be significant for large, complicated systems with significant filtration or distribution requirements: for instance, the installed cost for pumps, controls, filtration, and treatment can add thousands or tens of thousands to the cost of an active system, often representing an additional $2 - $5 per gallon of harvesting system capacity.

2.4.2 Operation and Maintenance

Rain barrels typically require little or no maintenance, and any maintenance that is required can be performed by the homeowner without significant cost.

Maintenance costs for active harvesting systems are generally low for well-designed systems. Recommended primary routine maintenance and corrective activities and costs associated with cisterns are listed in Table 2 and 3 below (WERF, 2009). These costs were obtained from the Water Environment Research Foundation's (WERF) BMP and LID Whole-Life Cost Model (average hourly labor rates and crew sizes are assumed for each activity). Note that in practice the frequency of these activities tends to vary. Additional maintenance activities may be needed depending on the intended use of harvested water and other site-specific conditions.

Table 2: Routine Maintenance Costs for Typical Cistern Systems (WERF*, 2009)

Routine Maintenance Activities	Months Between Events	Cost per Event	Total Cost per Year
Inspection, Reporting & Information Management	6	$ 130	$ 260
Roof Washing, Cleaning Inflow Filters	6	$ 240	$ 480

Table 3: Corrective and Infrequent Maintenance Costs for Typical Cistern Systems (WERF*, 2009)

Corrective and Infrequent Maintenance Activities (Unplanned and/or >3yrs. between events)	Years Between Events	Cost per Event	Total Cost per Year
Intermittent System Maintenance (System flush, debris/sediment removal from tank)	3	$ 390	$ 130
Pump Replacement	5	$ 989	$ 198

*References used by WERF in constructing these tables are identified in the 'References' section at the end of this document.

2.4.3 Programmatic

Among the biggest impediments to the expanded use of rainwater harvesting for water conservation and stormwater control is the perceived lack of economic benefit and inability to realize significant return on the substantial upfront cost of system installation, as well as relative newness of the practice for use in stormwater, which creates uncertainty on how to quantify and grant credit as a BMP. Researchers have cited the low water cost rates in the United States as compared to other countries as a major barrier to stormwater reuse (US EPA, 2006). Some policymakers have sought to address this issue by offering tax breaks and other economic incentives for rainwater harvesting installations. At the federal level, the American Recovery and Reinvestment Act (ARRA) of 2009 includes rainwater harvesting as one type of project that is considered eligible for funding. In addition, a number of states have tax credits, rebates, or grant programs to help finance rainwater harvesting projects. As mentioned previously, several major cities also offer credit or fee reductions through stormwater utilities to incentivize stormwater capture and use. While harvesting systems are typically more expensive than other stormwater BMPs on a per-gallon-of-runoff-mitigated basis, they offer a water conservation benefit that other stormwater BMPs do not.

To address the issue of water rates more directly, EPA has advocated "pricing water to accurately reflect the true costs of providing high quality water" as a means to "maintain infrastructure and encourage conservation" (USEPA, 2006). This "full cost" pricing would include the cost to collect, treat, and distribute water and would include capital, operation and maintenance, and energy costs. The use of full cost pricing "to encourage efficient use and conservation [of municipal water]," however, must be balanced with the need to provide "universal access for 'necessity' uses" (NRDC, 2011). To maintain the availability of affordable water to meet basic needs while encouraging the use of alternative water sources for high demand applications, some areas have implemented (or are considering) a tiered or block rate system for water pricing.

A typical block rate pricing structure sets water prices based on each user's water demand profile. Water demand is divided into blocks based on cumulative water consumption. The first block – consisting of the first 'X' gallons of water used in a month – is assigned the lowest unit cost ($/thousand gallons) depending on use or customer type. Any water use beyond the first block (e.g. greater than 'X' gallons) is assigned to the second block and priced at a higher rate; rates continue to increase as demand increases and more blocks are added. This type of pricing structure ensures that affordable water is available to meet basic needs, while high volume users are given incentive to seek alternative water sources to offset higher rates for excessive use (NRDC, 2011).

2.4.4 Predictability

The long-term cost-effectiveness and return on investment (ROI) for rainwater harvesting systems depend on a number of factors, and few cost-benefit analyses have been published to date. While a full cost-benefit analysis is beyond the scope of this report, the major issues requiring consideration in such an analysis are discussed below:

Capital Cost – The initial capital cost represents the primary cost factor associated with installing a rainwater harvesting system. This initial cost (along with additional costs associated with maintenance and permitting) is weighed against the present value of future benefits. Compounding the valuation of up-front investment in harvesting system equipment is the estimation of the life-cycle of its various components and the system overall. Consistent representation of life-cycle and mean-time-to-failure data of various wearing components (pumps, treatment systems, and filtration) would allow for better time-value assessment of up-front capital costs over the life of the system.

Maintenance Cost – As discussed previously, maintenance costs are incurred for routine and corrective maintenance performed over the life of the system. These costs are typically minimal for properly designed systems.

Water Conservation Benefit – According to a 2010 study conducted by the Low Impact Development Center, the current price of water in the U.S. ranges between $0.70 and $4 per 1,000 gallons with an average of $2.50. The potential for increasing water rates due to increased demand is often cited as one of the chief drivers for implementing rainwater harvesting, however, a quantitative financial assessment of water conservation benefits and therefore return on investment associated with implementing harvesting systems is based on an assumption of water costs over the life of the system. Coming to some rational projection for the escalation of water costs in a particular area over a 20 to 30 year period can be a matter of significant subjectivity. By example, in a 2010 article in the American Water Works Association Journal, Steve Maxwell cites several examples of rapidly increasing water prices over the last decade and predicts that this trend will continue and will extend to "more and more regions around the world" (Maxwell, 2010). Conversely, some public water suppliers project their water costs to increase at a rate of only 3% per year for the next 25 years. While this is a significant rate increase over that period, it is far below the double-digit annual increases experienced by some municipalities over the last 5 years. Clearly the potential for significant water rate increases is present, however this potential is very hard to characterize.

As a result, it can become difficult or impossible to resolve on water cost escalation factors on which a financial analysis would need to be based, resulting in an inability to objectively assess the financial benefits of harvesting as an alternative to centrally supplied water. When conservatively low escalation rates are applied, there rarely appears to be an economic basis for investing in harvesting system infrastructure. When reasonably high escalation rates are applied, systems may be built based on the promise of cost savings, but to date few systems have been monitored over sufficient time periods to demonstrate that such savings occur.

Stormwater Management Benefit – In the last decade, an increasing number of municipalities have implemented stormwater utilities and have established stormwater service fees to property owners separate from fees already in place for water and sewer services. In introducing this new fee structure, municipalities seek to increase awareness of the impacts of development on hydrology and system capacity, and the importance of managing the quantity and quality of stormwater runoff. To ease demands on downstream infrastructure and mitigate potential impacts on receiving streams, many municipalities offer credits (or fee reduction) against stormwater utility fees to property owners for on-site stormwater management. In cities such as Richmond, VA, cisterns are an approved BMP for reducing runoff quantity and improving runoff quality, which can result in a stormwater utility fee reduction of as much as 50%. Reductions in stormwater fees offer a tangible economic benefit for implementation of rainwater harvesting, which may significantly reduce payback times and lead to more widespread use.

Public Outreach and Sustainability Benefit – Increasing public awareness and advocacy of environmental programs such as the U.S. Green Building Council's (USGBC) Leadership in Energy and Environmental Design (LEED) program have created a public relations benefit for public and private entities that are viewed as environmentally responsible. The LEED program "promotes sustainable building and design practices through a suite of rating systems" which identify and award credit for sustainable design choices (USGBC, 2011). Included in the LEED rating system is a category for Water Efficiency, which includes credit for both stormwater management and water conservation. Rainwater harvesting systems are well-suited to achieving these Water Efficiency goals and can be used to achieve multiple LEED certification points. The USGBC reports that construction of green buildings has a number of tangible benefits to building owners including positive perception among consumers and potential customers and the ability to attract tenants and charge increased rental rates (USGBC, 2011).

Energy Use and Environmental Benefit – A significant amount of energy is required to extract, treat, and distribute water. Data from Mehan (2007) and the California Energy Commission indicate that "the water sector consumes 3% of the electricity generated in the U.S." and "decreasing water demand by 1 million gallons can reduce electricity use by nearly 1,500 kWh" (Kloss, 2008). This reduction in energy use also translates to reduced carbon emissions. Although difficult to quantify for individual system owners, the value of these benefits may be considered in a larger scale cost-benefit analysis of rainwater harvesting.

Cost Factors -- Links to Recommended Resources

Codes and Policy Documents:

United States Green Building Council (USGBC):

An Introduction to LEED

Guidance Materials

US EPA:

Water and Wastewater Pricing

Research Documents:

Water Environment Research Foundation (WERF):

BMP and LID Whole Life Cost Tools

Duke University (Hicks, 2008)

A Cost-Benefit Analysis of Rainwater Harvesting at Federal Facilities in Arlington County, Virginia

3. CONSIDERATIONS REQUIRING ADDITIONAL RESEARCH

Although a significant number of research papers and regulatory policies have been developed with regard to rainwater harvesting and stormwater reuse, there are several aspects of rainwater harvesting which may benefit from additional research or policy discussion:

Economics of Rainwater Harvesting – Few cost-benefit analyses of rainwater harvesting systems have been published to date. An analysis assessing the sensitivity to various parameters, including demand, cistern size, and water rates could indicate which measures are most likely to see a quicker payback period, as well as potentially identifying thresholds for each parameter that make ROI's particularly attractive.

A more comprehensive cost-benefit analysis would consider a number of complicated technical and socio-economic factors in addition to the primary considerations noted above, including potential increases in property value and assignment of monetary value to energy savings and reduced environmental impacts. Such an analysis would need to be conducted for a range of climate conditions and development types to better inform decisions about Return on Investment (ROI) and the economic viability of the practice.

Human Health Risks – As discussed previously, many existing regulations already address cross-connection and backflow prevention procedures to ensure separation of rainwater from the potable water supply. In most jurisdictions even rain barrels are required to be clearly labeled to reduce the risks of accidental ingestion. However, when it comes to requirements for treatment of harvested rainwater before use, little data is available to objectively assess the appropriate level of treatment needed for a given use and related human exposure. More detailed research regarding the health risks associated with ingestion of rainwater – and importantly, secondary exposures such as mists from irrigation system – and how these risks change depending on factors such as collection area, storage time, and filtration methods, may serve to inform future policy decisions about the acceptable treatment requirements and uses of harvested water as they relate to public health.

Regional and Climate Considerations – Rainfall patterns and climate conditions have a significant impact on the drivers and potential efficacy of rainwater harvesting. In arid areas of the United States, such as the Southwest, where rainfall occurs during a limited period of the year, water conservation and flood prevention may be primary drivers for stormwater capture and on-site use. Communities on the East Coast, however, may realize greater benefit from reduction of pollutant loads or mitigation of combined sewer overflows. A greater understanding of the regional factors associated with rainwater harvesting may help to shape policy decisions and encourage innovation to develop new technologies better suited to the needs and goals of a particular climate region.

Environmental and Ecological Impacts – Rainwater harvesting systems are an effective means for on-site stormwater management and are considered a Low Impact Development technique which helps to match the hydrology of developed land to the pre-development condition. Widespread use of this practice, however, particularly with indoor use of harvested water, may significantly alter the water balance of a site as compared to pre-development hydrology. Additional research is needed to assess the potential for hydrologic and ecological impacts due to reductions in infiltration, evapotranspiration, and groundwater recharge associated with on-site use of harvested stormwater as compared to other stormwater management techniques.

4. SUMMARY AND RECOMMENDATIONS

This report summarizes the results of a literature review of the research and policy documents representing the current state of the practice in rainwater harvesting in the areas of water conservation, stormwater volume and pollutant load reduction, code, and administration and cost factors.

The key findings from this review and recommendations for future research are summarized below.

4.1   Findings

While the technical and maintenance aspects of rainwater harvesting in each of these topic areas have been well documented in state guidance manuals and other available research, relatively few states have published such manuals and many states have no clearly established regulations governing rainwater harvesting.

In many areas of the country, significant progress has been made at the municipal level to codify, permit, and incentivize the use of rainwater harvesting for both water conservation and stormwater management.

State and local codes addressing rainwater harvesting, while generally similar, tend to vary somewhat in the level of detail provided, particularly as related to cross-connection/backflow prevention requirements, treatment requirements, and associated acceptable uses of harvested water. Regulations addressing the use of rainwater harvesting as a stormwater BMP are generally better defined and more consistent from place to place.

At present, the most prominent driver for broad implementation of rainwater harvesting appears to be stormwater runoff and pollutant load reduction due to the regulatory and financial incentives offered by state environmental agencies and local stormwater utilities.

New control technologies enable the autonomous operation of such systems and provide an opportunity for improved performance of harvesting systems in stormwater control.

Although the water conservation benefits associated with harvesting systems are significant, the availability of low-cost centrally-supplied water throughout much of the United States and other developed countries mitigates the economic benefits associated with water conservation. For example, a 3,200-gallon cistern designed based on the WERF whole-life cost analysis tool to collect runoff for a 1-inch storm event on a 5,000 ft^2 roof collection area would have a total life cycle cost of about $31,000 (net present value). Based solely on water conservation benefit (assuming an average municipal water cost of $2.50 per 1,000 gallons), this system would require the tank to fill with rainwater and be completely drawn down over 3,800 times for payback to be achieved. Note that this payback period is based on the assumption of current average municipal water rates. As mentioned previously, increases in water rates or the implementation of block-based pricing may make rainwater harvesting more cost effective.

The absence of detailed, long-term cost-benefit analyses represents a significant gap in available research related to rainwater harvesting systems.

4.2   Recommendations

National standards, such as the GPMCS, may provide a guide for defining a minimum standard of care in the design of rainwater harvesting systems. If adopted by state and local governments, such codes may help to ensure a level of consistency in local codes across different locations.

A comprehensive cost-benefit analysis conducted for several different climate regions and development types, considering capital and maintenance costs, water rates, stormwater regulations and fees, property values, energy savings, and environmental impacts may provide useful insight into the economic viability of rainwater harvesting practices.

Development of full-cost pricing guidelines of centrally supplied water, including embedded energy-water attributes, will provide a basis of comparison for alternative water supplies such as harvesting systems.

More detailed investigations of human exposure paths and associated health risks, climate factors, and potential ecological impacts of rainwater harvesting are also recommended.

5. CASE STUDIES

Under the scope of this Task Order, the Project Team conducted a literature review of existing research and policy documents related to rainwater harvesting, with particular focus on characterizing the current state of the practice in the areas of: (1) water conservation, (2) stormwater volume and pollutant load reduction, (3) code and administration considerations, and (4) cost factors.

Attached to this report are five case studies covering these topic areas that provide examples of site specific applications of water reuse through stormwater capture. The case studies include project specific information including: type of demand or use (i.e. irrigation, toilet flushing, etc.), type of project (i.e. public or private), whether the project is new construction or a retrofit, key project benefits, and, where available, projected water savings. Figures included in the case studies illustrate different elements in the rainwater harvesting systems, from above ground cisterns to underground modular tank systems. The purpose of the case studies is to showcase how rainwater harvesting can be used to promote sustainability and meet project goals.

6. REFERENCES

American Rainwater Catchment Systems Association (ARCSA)/American Society of Plumbing Engineers (ASPE). *Rainwater Catchment Design and Installation Standards*. Austin, TX. October 2008.

American Water Works Association (AWWA). *Commercial and Institutional End Uses of Water*. Denver, CO. AWWA, 2000. <http://www.waterrf.org/ProjectsReports/PublicReportLibrary/RFR90806_2000_241B.pdf>. (Accessed November 2011).

American Water Works Association (AWWA). *Residential End Uses of Water*, Denver, CO. AWWA, 1999.

American Water Works Association (AWWA). "Water Use Statistics." <http://www.drinktap.org/consumerdnn/Home/WaterInformation/Conservation/WaterUseStatistics/tabid/85/Default.aspx>. (Accessed July 2011).

Boller, M. Tracking heavy metals reveals sustainability deficits of urban drainage systems. *Water Science Technology* 35(9): 77-87. 1997.

Cabell Brand Center. Virginia Rainwater Harvesting Manual, Second Edition. Salem, VA. July 2009.

City of Chicago. "Chicago Sustainable Backyard Program." <http://www.cityofchicago.org/city/en/depts/doe/provdrs/nat_res/svcs/how_can_i_get_a_rainbarrelorcompostbinrebateform.html>. (Accessed July 2011).

City of Los Angeles Department of Public Works. *City of Los Angeles Rainwater Harvesting Program: A Homeowner's "How-To" Guide*. Los Angeles. November 2009. <http://larainwaterharvesting.org/images/Homeowner_How-To_Guide.pdf>. (Accessed July 2011).

City of Minneapolis. "Minneapolis Stormwater Utility Fee." <http://www.ci.minneapolis.mn.us/stormwater/fee/index.asp>. (Accessed July 2011).

City of Portland. *One and Two Family Dwelling Specialty Code*. Portland, OR. March 2001. <http://www.portlandonline.com/shared/cfm/image.cfm?id=68627>. (Accessed July 2011).

City of Richmond Department of Public Utilities. *Non-Residential & Multi-Family Property Credit Manual*. Richmond, VA. February, 2011.

City and County of San Francisco. Memorandum of Understanding Between: San Francisco Public Utilities Commission (SFPUC) & San Francisco Department of Building Inspection (DBI) & San Francisco Department of Public Health (DPH) For: Permitting Requirements for Rainwater Harvesting Systems Located Within the City and County of San Francisco. San Francisco. June 2008.

City of Tucson. City of Tucson Water Harvesting Guidance Manual, Ordinance Number 10210. Tucson, AZ. October 2005.

Clark, S.E., K.A. Steele, J. Spicher, C.Y.S. Siu, M.M. Lalor, R. Pitt, J.T. Kirby. Roofing materials' contributions to stormwater runoff pollution. *Journal of Irrigation and Drainage Engineering* 134(5):638-645. 2008.

County of Los Angeles Department of Public Health. Policy No. 515.07: Approval and Use of Cisterns for Rainfall/Runoff Capture and Distribution. Los Angeles, CA. January 2010.

Ecker, Susan R. *Rainwater Harvesting and the Plumbing Codes*, Plumbing Engineer, March 2007. <http://www.plumbingengineer.com/march_07/rainwater.php>. (Accessed November 2011).

Forasté, A., and Hirschman, D. A Methodology for Using Rainwater Harvesting as a Stormwater Management BMP. Conference Proceedings, 2010 Low Impact Development Conference. <http://www.cwp.org/cbstp/Resources/d3s3a-asce.pdf>. (Accessed November 2011).

Georgia Department of Community Affairs. *Georgia Rainwater Harvesting Guidelines*. Atlanta, GA. 2009. <http://www.dca.state.ga.us/development/constructioncodes/programs/downloads/GeorgiaRain WaterHarvestingGuidelines_2009.pdf>. (Accessed July 2011).

Gold, A., Goo, R., Hair, L., Arazan, N. "Rainwater Harvesting: Policy, Programs, and Practices for Water Supply Sustainability." *Low Impact Development: Redefining Water in the City*. pp. 987- 1002. ASCE, 2010.

Hauber-Davidson, G. "Supplementing Urban Water Supplies Through Industrial and Commercial Rainwater Harvesting Schemes". Water Conservation Group, Pymble/Sydney NSW, Australia. <www.watergroup.com.au/download/P_RWH-integrUrbWatSuplyGHDv1a070308.pdf>. (Accessed June 2012).

Hicks, Bill. "A Cost Benefit Analysis of Rainwater Harvesting at Commercial Facilities in Arlington County, Virginia." Duke University. 2008. <http://dukespace.lib.duke.edu/dspace/bitstream/10161/512/1/MP_wdh11_a_200805.pdf>. (Accessed July 2011).

Hunt, W. and L. Szpir. "Permeable Pavements, Green Roofs, and Cisterns." UrbanWaterways Publication Series. North Carolina Cooperative Extension Service. 2006.

Illinois State Senate. "State Bill 38: Rainwater Harvesting for Non-Potable Uses." <http://www.ilga.gov/legislation/fulltext.asp?DocName=&SessionId=84&GA=97&DocTypeId= SB&DocNum=38&GAID=11&LegID=54559&SpecSess=&Session= >. (Accessed November 2011).

International Association of Plumbing and Mechanical Officials (IAPMO). *Green Plumbing & Mechanical Supplement.* Ontario, CA. November 2010.

Kloss, Chris. "Managing Wet Weather with Green Infrastructure Municipal Handbook." December 2008. <http://www.epa.gov/npdes/pubs/gi_munichandbook_harvesting.pdf>. (Accessed July 2011).

Liaw, C., and Y. Tsai. Optimum storage volume of rooftop rainwater harvesting systems for domestic use. *Journal of the American Water Resources Association* 40(4):902-912. 2004.

Maxwell, Steve. "Historical Water Price Trends." *American Water Works Association Journal.* AWWA, 2010.

Mehan, G.T. Energy, Climate Change, and Sustainable Water Management. *Environment Reporter – The Bureau of National Affairs*, 38(48). December 7, 2007.

Morales, M.A., Martin, J.M., Heaney, J.P. "Methods for Estimating Commercial, Industrial, and Institutional Water Use." Fall 2009 FSAWWA Water Conference. Orlando, FL. 2009.

Natural Resources Defense Council (NRDC). *Capturing Rainwater from Rooftops: An Efficient Water Resource Management Strategy that Increases Supply and Reduces Pollution.* November 2011. < http://www.nrdc.org/water/rooftoprainwatercapture.asp>. (Accessed December 2011).

New York City Department of Environmental Protection. *NYC Green Infrastructure Plan.* New York. September 2010. <http://www.nyc.gov/html/dep/html/stormwater/nyc_green_infrastructure_plan.shtml>. (Accessed July 2011).

North Carolina Department of Water Quality (NC DWQ). *Technical Guidance: Stormwater Treatment Credit for Rainwater Harvesting Systems.* September 2008. <http://h2o.enr.state.nc.us/su/documents/RainwaterHarvesting_Approved.pdf>. (Accessed November 2011).

Pacific Institute. Waste Not, Want Not: The Potential for Urban Water Conservation in California. Oakland, CA. November 2003. <http://www.pacinst.org/reports/urban_usage/waste_not_want_not_full_report.pdf>. (Accessed July 2011).

Philadelphia Water Department: Office of Watersheds. "Green City, Clean Waters: Combined Sewer Overflow Long Term Control Plan Update." <http://www.phillywatersheds.org/what_were_doing/documents_and_data/cso_long_term_contr ol_plan>. (Accessed July 2011).

Pitt, R., Clark, S., Talebi, L., Bean, R. *Stormwater Non-Potable Beneficial Uses and Effects on Urban Infrastructure.* Water Environment Research Foundation (WERF). 2011. <http://www.iwapublishing.com/template.cfm?name=isbn9781780400365>.

Texas Rainwater Harvesting Evaluation Committee. *Rainwater Harvesting Potential and Guidelines for Texas*, Report to the 80th Legislature. Austin, TX. November 2006.

Texas Water Development Board (TWDB). *Texas Manual on Rainwater Harvesting, Third Edition.* Austin, TX. 2005.

Thomas, Terry. *RWH Performance Predictor for Use with Coarse (i.e. Monthly) Rainfall Data, RN-RWH04.* Development Technology Unit, School of Engineering at the University of Warwick, Domestic Roofwater Harvesting Research Programme. 2004.

Traugott, Alan. *Reclaimed Water and the Codes*, Consulting-Specifying Engineer, April 1, 2007. <http://www.csemag.com/index.php?id=1398&cHash=081010&tx_ttnews[tt_news]=22634>. (Accessed November 2011).

U.S. Environmental Protection Agency (USEPA), *Water & Wastewater Pricing,* December 18, 2006. <http://water.epa.gov/infrastructure/sustain/Water-and-Wastewater-Pricing-Introduction.cfm>. (Accessed November 2011).

United States Green Building Council (USGBC). "An Introduction to LEED." <http://www.usgbc.org/DisplayPage.aspx?CMSPageID=1988>. (Accessed July 2011).

Van Metre, P.C., and B.J. Mahler. The contribution of particles washed from rooftops to contaminant loading to urban streams. *Chemosphere* 52:1727-1741. 2003.

Virginia Department of Conservation and Recreation (VADCR). *Stormwater Design Specification No. 6.* March 2011. <http://vwrrc.vt.edu/swc/april_22_2010_update/DCR_BMP_Spec_No_6_RAINWATER_HARVESTING_Final_Draft_v1-8_04132010.htm>. (Accessed July 2011).

Water Environment Research Foundation (WERF). *BMP and LID Whole Life Cost Models, Version 2.*0. Alexandria, VA. 2009. <http://www.werf.org/AM/Template.cfm?Section=Research_Profile&Template=/CustomSource/Research/PublicationProfile.cfm&id=SW2R08>.

References Cited by WERF Cost Model:

Canada Freshwater Management (CFM). *Retrofit.* <http://www.ec.gc.ca/Water/en/manage/effic/e_retro.htm>. (Accessed October 2008).

Cengel, Y., and Cimbala, J. Fluid Mechanics, Fundamentals and Applications (2nd Ed.). Boston, MA: McGraw- Hill. 2006.

Darco Underground Tankage, Inc. *Underground Tank Project Estimate.* <http://www.darcoinc.com/TankQuote.php>. (Accessed December 2008).

Hicks, Bill. *A Cost-Benefit Analysis of Rainwater Harvesting at Commercial Facilities in Arlington County, Virginia.* <http://dukespace.lib.duke.edu/dspace/bitstream/10161/512/1/MP_wdh11_a_200805.pdf>. (Accessed October 2008).

Miller, M. Personal communication Oct. 2008 with Mark Miller, Owner of Mark Miller Toyota concerning the cistern installation at his dealership. Salt Lake City, UT.

Nicklas, M. *Rainwater, the Untapped Resource.* High Performance Buildings Online Magazine. <http://www.hpbmagazine.org/images/stories/articles/Rainwater.pdf>. (Accessed October 2008).

Ohio State Extension. On-Site Sprinkler Irrigation of Treated Wastewater in Ohio. *Bulletin number 912*, Ohio State University. < http://ohioline.osu.edu/b912/step_5.html>. (Accessed Oct. 2008).

UC Berkley. *Water Audit Summary.* <http://sustainability.berkeley.edu/water_plan/Summary_Res_Hall_Audit.pdf\>. (Accessed October 2008).

R.S. Means estimate compiled by Construction Control Corporation, Salt Lake City, UT.